SOLUTIONS TO EMOTIONAL PROBLEMS

KEY WAYS TO RECOVER FROM HEARTBREAK AND OTHER EMOTIONAL ISSUES

JEFFERY HUNTERS

Table of Contents

INTRODUCTION

We all naturally and fundamentally care about our health. It's a dynamic process that constantly evolves. It is a blessing and a necessity to be healthy. A person in good health may accomplish more in less time and does not avoid their responsibilities. He is capable of doing reasonable work and never procrastinates. His work is energized and strengthened by good health. He enjoys every aspect of life, including the food he eats. If we take ownership of our wellness, we may manage career success, physical activity, emotional difficulties, and stress coping. Wellness is an improvement in quality of life with personal growth or positive behaviors and attitude.

A priceless blessing in life is having good health. Maintain it by physical activity, a morning stroll, play, a balanced diet, adequate rest, and the avoidance of stress. Disorders occur when we lose control over our health and become careless with our meals or sleep. A mental disorder is a psychological condition that can develop as a result of negligence. This has an impact on intellectual development and learning capacity. A mental disorder is a mental condition that affects a person's behavior, emotions, and mood. Everyone of us occasionally feels unhappy, happy, healthy, or ill, and occasionally it lasts for a day, week, or month. If these sentiments conflict with these ideas, a mental or emotional problem may be present.

Disorders that start in childhood or adolescence might last years without a diagnosis or treatment. The emotional chaos is a type of mental condition when there is some degree of emotional disturbance brought on by anomalies in brain development or function. A psychological problem exists if your emotions and feelings are not in the appropriate state. If a person's personality is plainly displayed by their overly dramatic behavior and overly emotional thoughts, this is a definite sign of an emotional disorder.

There is a correlation between emotional illnesses and specific causes like physical abuse, poverty, neglect, parental stress, unreasonable expectations, rule changes, confusions, and so on. Here, we outline eight emotional issues that we could encounter on a regular basis along with their answers.

One of the pressing emotional issues is **depression**.

OVERCOMING DEPRESSION

People who are depressed have a brief episode of the blues. Depression is a state of extreme sadness, helplessness, and hopelessness. You are beneath the heavy shadow of something. Depression is generally treated since it provides you a sense of purpose in life. Do not be embarrassed to ask for assistance if this is keeping you from sleeping. It may also contribute to the side effects of medications, including those for high blood pressure or sleeping aids. Due to this dismal mood, a patient with depression seeks out drugs, and in some extreme circumstances, it results in suicide. Depression can be treated with psychotherapy, medications, healthy eating, exercise, good sleep habits, and life planning.

OVERCOMING PHOBIA

A phobia is an unreasonable fear of a particular object. Most people only have modest worries, but when they intensify, they cause considerable anxiety and disrupt daily living. Fears of heights, tight quarters, snakes, needles, etc. are common. All of these are largely treatable. The majority of youngsters who develop phobias experience life-changing effects. A severe phobia is when you experience every fear, which is extreme and genuinely incurable. It will actively pursue suicidal behavior. The only way to treat it is to do it on your own or to realize your own inner strength. The patient with phobia can benefit from behavior therapy, counter conditioning, and a structured treatment procedure.

One of the most obvious emotional disorders is emotional eating.

emotional eating.

We start overeating or undereating because of mixed emotions or worries when we are emotionally upset or unable to articulate our sentiments. Emotional eating can be difficult to diagnose. Stress-related emotional eating, according to psychologists, contributes to obesity. Anger, guilt, shame, loneliness, fear, boredom—these are all causes of emotional eating, which is unhealthy for the body and low in nutrients. How to quit for everyone is the issue that has to be addressed more. The coping mechanism only functions in this circumstance. The treatment for stopping eating and focusing on other essentials of life is motivation and sharing your thoughts or feelings.

Stubbornness

Fear of losing something can lead to stubbornness, an emotional condition that makes a person dogmatic about everything in his life. The greatest treatment for this emotional behavior is counseling. Many individuals find the word "stubbornness" to be very difficult to use and describe it as prideful, rebellious, disloyal, greedy, and defiant, all of which are accurate depending on your perspective. People sometimes employ improper defensive strategies to justify their rigidity. In order to get it treated, a person must speak with a counselor.

Hyper-sensitivity

Although being sensitive is not wrong, being overly sensitive will get you into a lot of difficulty. It's okay to display your emotional side. But occasionally, some people experience intense emotion. Being too sensitive has many benefits. Similarly, these people are goal-oriented, but they also have a lot of defects. Most hypersensitive people overwork. They end up taking on too much, which causes them to suffer at the end of the day.

They frequently become anxious rapidly. Numerous issues are brought on by it, including migraines, depression, and headaches. By practicing meditation, listening to soothing music, and striking a balance between many activities, one can get rid of their hypersensitivity.

Isolation

You begin to experience loneliness at some time in life. For a while, you cut yourself off from the outside world. It is perfectly natural for any individual, but if it keeps happening to you, it indicates that you are isolated. Bullying at school, low self-esteem, worry about losing friends, worry about getting wounded, etc. are a few of the causes. It is a mental state in which you nearly become lost. In this circumstance, a person begins to doubt his life and believes he is unworthy. Even when they cut themselves off from the outside world, the condition can sometimes worsen to the point where some people consider suicide.

There are ways to deal with this emotional issue, and one of them is to reconnect with old friends. A person can join online communities and participate in various discussions if they don't feel comfortable with their friends. Going to a park and experiencing nature is another method for solving the issue. You become calmer the more time you spend in nature. When you are tranquil, you stop wondering about life and begin to appreciate it. An individual can overcome their solitude by having a pet. You get the opportunity to interact with a pet and feel its love.

One of the most ignored emotional issues is aggression.

aggression.

The term "aggression" is used to describe those who hurt themselves or other people. There are several types of aggression. It may be verbal, emotional, mental, or physical. There are several contributing elements. Sometimes a person's upbringing is the root of their hostility. A person becomes hostile when they feel neglected or when they are verbally abused. Parenting is not the only factor contributing to the intense degree of emotions; occasionally, a traumatic event also plays a role.

Even if it can be fixed, the aggressive individual needs to be dealt with in a very calm manner. You should give someone room if they get hostile. A person with high energy levels has poor impulse control and may hurt themselves. Don't say anything that makes their predicament worse. Contacting a physician or a psychiatrist is crucial. He may suggest some drugs that will aid in the condition's recovery. The drugs specifically target the brain's neurotransmitters, which aids in relaxing the brain cells.

Fear Attacks

It is a condition in which a person experiences extreme levels of fear and anxiety, making it difficult for them to breathe. You could be struck by a ferocious wave of terror at any time without exhibiting any symptoms. Although the primary cause of a panic attack is yet unknown, any distressing event might occasionally serve as the trigger.

The patient must practice deep breathing techniques to treat this condition. You gain control over your response to various situations when you learn to control your breathing. It has been demonstrated that lavender can treat panic attacks. If you carry lavender oil, you can apply it to your hands during a panic attack and breathe in the aroma. It will be partially treated.

EMOTIONAL INTELLIGENCE

Your future promotion might not be assured by the technical abilities that helped you land your first one. You should take into account the emotional component if you want to hold a leadership position. It enables you to collaborate with others, offer feedback, manage stress, and coach teams effectively.

Nearly 90% of what distinguishes top performers from colleagues with equivalent technical abilities and knowledge is emotional intelligence.

Emotional intelligence: What Is It?

Understanding and controlling your own emotions as well as being able to identify and affect the emotions of those around you are all examples of having emotional intelligence. Researchers John Mayer and Peter Salovey first used the term in 1990, but psychologist Daniel Goleman later made it more well-known.

In a statement to the Harvard Business Review from more than ten years ago, Goleman emphasized the significance of emotional intelligence in leadership. He said that "the most successful leaders are all alike in one crucial way: They all have a high degree of what has come to be known as emotional intelligence. Not that intelligence and technical proficiency are unimportant. They are important, but they are also the prerequisites for executive roles.

Emotional intelligence, commonly referred to as EQ, has developed into a necessary talent over time. Emotional intelligence, according to research by EQ provider TalentSmart, is the best indicator of performance. Recruiters have taken note, too: According to a CareerBuilder survey, 71% of employers said they valued EQ over IQ, noting that people with high emotional intelligence are more likely to remain composed under stress, handle conflict diplomatically, and show empathy for their coworkers.

THE EMOTIONAL INTELLIGENCE'S FOUR PARTS

Four main competencies are commonly used to describe emotional intelligence:

Self-awareness

Self-management

Social conscience

Relationship control

It's critical to comprehend what each component comprises if you want to raise your emotional intelligence. The four categories are described in further detail below:

Awareness of Oneself

Self-awareness is the foundation of all things. It reflects your capacity to detect your emotions and the impact they have on your performance and the performance of your team, in addition to your understanding of your strengths and shortcomings.

95 percent of people believe they are self-aware, but only 10 to 15 percent actually are, according to study by organizational psychologist Tasha Eurich, which might cause issues for your employees. Working with coworkers who lack self-awareness can significantly reduce a team's success and, in Eurich's research, increase stress and deplete motivation.

Self-awareness is important because it helps you realize your own potential before you can help others do the same. By completing 360-degree feedback, in which you evaluate your performance and compare it to the views of your employer, peers, and direct reports, you can quickly gauge your level of self-awareness. You will learn about your own behavior through this process, as well as about how you are viewed within the company.

Self-Management

Self-management is the capacity to control your emotions, particularly under pressure, and to keep a positive attitude in the face of obstacles. Lacking self-control, leaders are more likely to react and struggle to control their emotions.

Reactions frequently occur automatically. But the easier it is for you to switch from reaction to response, the more emotionally intelligent you are. In order to respond to stress and adversity more effectively and deliberately, it's critical to remember to take a moment to halt, breathe, gather your thoughts, and do whatever it takes to control your emotions. This may involve going for a walk or calling a friend.

Social Sensitivity

Understanding and controlling your own emotions are crucial, but you also need to be able to read a room. Your capacity to discern the feelings of others and the organizational dynamics at work is referred to as social awareness.

Empathy is a skill that socially adept leaders use. They make an effort to comprehend the thoughts and viewpoints of their coworkers so they may interact and work together more successfully.

Empathy is the top leadership skill according to the global leadership development company DDI. Leaders who have mastered empathy outperform others by more than 40% when teaching, engaging people, and making decisions. Researchers from the Center for Creative Leadership found in a different study (pdf) that managers' bosses see them as better performers when they demonstrate greater empathy for their direct subordinates.

Empathic communication will help you to support your team more effectively while also enhancing your own performance.

Relationship Administration

Relationship management is the capacity to persuade, coach, mentor, and successfully resolve disagreement with others.

While some people want to avoid conflict, it's crucial to effectively handle problems when they come up. According to research, every unresolved argument can cost the organization eight hours in gossip and other unproductive activities, depleting resources and morale.

You must have those difficult conversations if you want to maintain the happiness of your team: According to a recent poll by the Society for Human Resource Management, "respectful treatment of all employees at all levels" was cited as the most important component in job satisfaction by 72% of respondents.

THE IMPORTANCE OF EMOTIONAL INTELLIGENCE

Leaders determine the atmosphere of their group. Lack of emotional intelligence could have more serious repercussions, such as reduced employee engagement and a higher likelihood of attrition.

Technical prowess is one thing, but if you can't work well with others or communicate with your team, people will overlook your technical prowess. You may develop your career and company by mastering emotional intelligence.

www.ingramcontent.com/pod-product-compliance
Lightning Source LLC
LaVergne TN
LVHW020547160826
845677LV00015B/4247

* 9 7 9 8 8 4 6 4 4 6 4 6 5 *